SNAP SHOT™

Senior Editor Mary Ling
Designer Joanna Pocock
Editor Finbar Hawkins
Production Catherine Semark

A SNAPSHOT™ BOOK

SNAPSHOT™ is an imprint of Covent Garden Books.
95 Madison Avenue
New York, NY 10016

ISBN 1-56458-732-0

Color reproduction by Colourscan
Printed and bound in Belgium by Proost

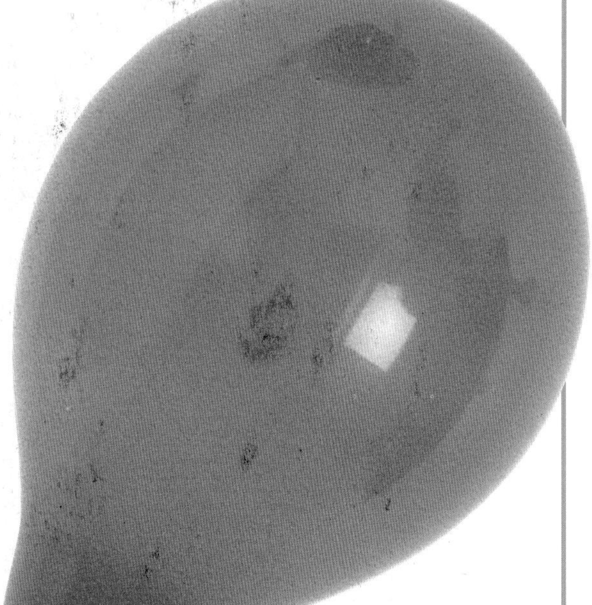

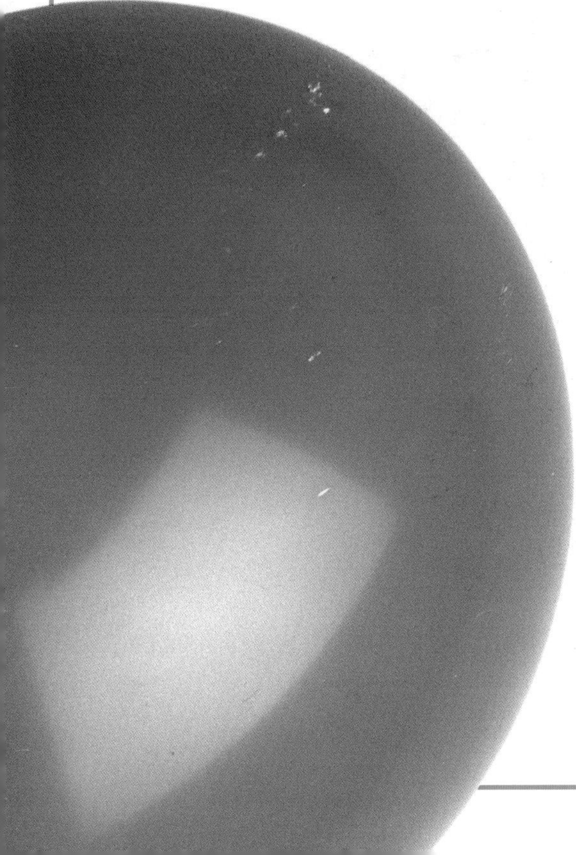

Would you

Do you
look into
the sky and
wish you could
fly like a kite or
float like a feather?

In the Air

Contents

like to fly?

Flying creatures, such
as birds and insects,
have wings and bodies
that are specially made
for life in the air.

Why are your wings

These butterflies
have brilliantly
colored wings,
which they
close up
when they
rest.

so bright, butterfly?

Their wings help hide them among flowers and are a colorful way to attract a mate.

What makes a

Insects do not dare
take to the air if
dragonflies are
around.

is whose?

4

5

6

Answers on page 32

31

Answers

1. Pigeon
2. Butterfly
3. Moth
4. Bat
5. Cricket
6. Owl